fly me to the moon
AF426027

First Published in April 2023

ISBN: 978-93-5741-771-6

BLUEROSE PUBLISHERS

www.BlueRoseONE.com
info@bluerosepublishers.com
+91 8882 898 898

Cover & Typographic Design:
Lynn Angela Rebello

Distributed by: BlueRose, Amazon, Flipkart

Fly me to the moon

Lynn Angela Rebello

To all the little ones with wild imaginations,
May this book inspire your own poetic creations.
This book is dedicated to the dreamers, the believers,
The ones who see magic in everyday endeavors.

May these pages be a portal to new worlds of fun,
Where laughter, adventure, and learning are never done.
Thank you for joining me on this journey of rhyme,
May these poems be a part of your childhood sublime.

So let's turn the page and explore together,
The wonder of words, and all they can conjure.
Let's make memories, and cherish each line,
For in the world of poetry, anything is possible and divine.

Contents

The Moon's Luminous Glow on the Ocean Below

Oh, the moon, so bright and round,
It shines on the sea, without a sound.
And all the creatures, in the deep blue,
Look up and wonder, at this shiny view.

The octopus dances, with its eight arms,
As the moonlight casts, its glittering charms.
The fish swim around, in a playful mood,
And the starfish glow, like little jewels.

The crabs scuttle on the sandy floor,
As the moonbeams shine, through the ocean's door.
And the dolphins jump, with graceful ease,
As the moon illuminates, the endless seas.

The sea creatures sing, a gentle tune,
To the moon, that smiles, on this lagoon.
They thank it, for this magical night,
And for shining its light, so bright.

For the moon, and the sea creatures below,
Are connected, by a luminous glow.
A bond that's timeless, and oh so true,
A reminder, that the world's beauty, is not just a few.

So little one, next time you look up at the moon,
Think of the sea creatures, in their underwater lagoon
For they too, marvel at this celestial sight,
And celebrate, the moon's beauty, with all their might.

The Pink Cow's Beauty

In the green meadows grazes a cow
With a coat as pink as the sunset glow
The other cows are brown and black
But this one stands out in the pack

She's a curious sight to behold
With her pink hide that's soft and bold
She munches on grass with delight
As she basks in the warm sunlight

The other cows sometimes stare
Wondering how she got that hair
But the pink cow just goes on grazing
Her beauty and grace never fading

In a field of green, she's a rose
A sight that nobody ever knows
But to those who take the time to see
A pink cow is a thing of beauty

So let's celebrate this creature rare
With her pink coat beyond compare
For in this world of brown and black
A pink cow is a treasure we can't lack.

The Love and Loyalty of a Dog

A dog and a human,
A bond like no other.
A friendship that lasts,
Forever and ever.

Through wagging of tails,
And playful barks too.
A dog's love is unconditional,
It's always true blue.

A human's companion,
A loyal furry friend.
A confidant, a protector,
Until the very end.

So treasure your pup,
With all of your heart.
For the love of a dog,
Is the sweetest of art.

I can't understand this
Embracing Our Flaws: A Celebration of Uniqueness
7

Flaws, oh flaws, they're not so bad,
In fact, they make us who we are, a tad.
No one's perfect, everyone has them too,
So let's embrace our flaws, me and you.

Maybe you have a birthmark on your cheek,
Or a scar that looks like a creek.
Maybe you're clumsy, and trip and fall,
Or have trouble with math, and that's not all.

But these things don't define who you are,
They're just a small part, like a shining star.
In fact, they make you special and unique,
A one-of-a-kind masterpiece, so to speak.

So let's embrace our flaws, and hold them dear,
For they make us special, that much is clear.
And know that you're loved, just as you are,
Flaws and all, like a shining star.

Fish in the Forest: A Magical Aquatic Wonderland

In a stream, deep in the wood,
A secret world, misunderstood.
Fish with fins, so bright and bold,
Swimming in a forest, untold.

Their scales shine, like jewels rare,
Darting through the water, with flair.
Colors galore, in shades so bright,
A mesmerizing, captivating sight.

They play hide-and-seek, among the leaves,
In their woodland home, where magic weaves.
Through the currents, they dance and glide,
A breathtaking show, with nature as their guide.

So if you venture, to the forest deep,
Look closely in the water's keep.
You might just glimpse, a fishy show,
In the forest's aquatic glow.

For nature's wonders, are vast and wide,
A treasure trove, with mysteries to confide.
And in the forest's watery embrace,
The fish swim freely, in a magical place.
So take a moment, and be still,
To marvel at nature's endless thrill.
With fish in the forest, a captivating scene,
A treasure of nature, evergreen! For in the woods,
where the trees stand tall,
Lives a world of fish, for one and all.
A wonderland, so pure and mild,
A precious gem, for every child. So let your imagination soar,
And explore the forest's watery floor.

Mother's Tales of Disney Magic

In Mother's stories, magic blooms,
With Disney characters, in their rooms.
Cinderella's glass slipper, so divine,
Snow White's poison apple, a warning sign.

A mermaid with a voice so pure,
A beast transformed, love to endure.
A fairy with a wand that gleams,
Tinkling pixie dust, in dreams.

Peter Pan and Neverland's flight,
A genie granting wishes bright.
Mickey Mouse's cheerful smile,
Bringing joy that lasts a while.

With Mother's tales, a world of wonder,
Where dreams come true, like thunder.
Enchanted lands and fairytales,
In Mother's stories, where magic prevails.

So snuggle close, my dear and near,
As Mother's tales, fill your ears.
Imagination takes its flight,
In a world of Disney's sheer delight.

Wizard Drew and his Kind Heart

There once was a
wizard named Drew,
With a cloak and a
hat that were blue,
He'd cast spells with
a wink,
And make potions
that stink,
But his heart was
always kind and
true!

BE GENTLE
WITH
YOURSELF
LOVE
yourself

There once was a person
named me
Who learned to love
themselves, you see
They looked in the mirror
And said with a cheer
"I'm worthy of love and
glee!"

Cherish Your Body: A Tribute to Self-Love

Your body, a temple of grace
A place to cherish, to embrace
Feed it with wholesome, nourishing meals
And see how your wellness reveals

Love yourself, just the way you are
Your beauty shines like a star
Flaunt your curves and your flaws
They're unique, they're your own applause

Take care of your body and soul
And see how your spirit unfolds
Move, dance, breathe and rest
And witness how your life is blessed

Nourish yourself with self-love
It's a gift from the heavens above
Your body is a precious treasure
Cherish it always, now and forever.

Bathroom Musings

The bathroom is a place we go
To take care of things we all know
But sometimes in this quiet space
Our minds can drift to a different place

As we sit and ponder on the throne
Our thoughts can wander on their own
To places far and wide, it seems
Like floating on a river in our dreams

We may be physically in the loo
But mentally we can travel anew
To a land of magic and wonder
A place where our minds can truly wander

So let us embrace these moments of rest
And allow our minds to be truly blessed
With dreams and visions that bring us joy
And give our hearts a chance to employ

The power of imagination and thought
That in the bathroom, we've all sought
So let us dream, and let us be
In this sacred place of privacy.

Sibling Love

Brother and sister, hand in hand,
Together they conquer, they understand,
Their love is strong, their bond is tight,
They stand together, through day and night.

Through thick and thin, they support each other,
With gentle words and comforting cover,
They share their secrets and their dreams,
And always know what each other means.

Their love is pure, their hearts entwined,
Brother and sister, two of a kind,
Their journey's long, but they'll never part,
For their love is forever in their heart.

You're More Than You Think
I believe in me

Once there was a tiny seed,
Buried deep in the soil's bed,
It dreamed of soaring up so high,
And reaching for the bright blue sky.

But day after day it stayed in place,
And nothing seemed to change its fate,
It wondered why it was stuck down low,
When all around it flowers grow.

One day a gentle rain began to fall,
And soon the seed began to sprawl,
It pushed its way up through the ground,
And a sprout emerged, healthy and sound.

With each new day it grew and grew,
And soon it was a flower in full bloom,
It smiled and stretched towards the sun,
Its life had only just begun.

The moral of this story is clear,
Just like the seed we all have fear,
But if we have patience and believe,
We can achieve what we truly conceive.

So dream big and never give up hope,
For one day you too will learn to cope,
And grow into the person you want to be,
A beautiful flower, wild and free.

I am beautiful

I am beautiful, just as I am,
With all my flaws and imperfections at hand,
My unique features and my quirks,
Are what make me special, not just a perk.

My beauty shines from deep within,
It's not just about the color of my skin,
It's in my smile and in my heart,
And it's something that sets me apart.

So when I look in the mirror and see,
A reflection of who I'm meant to be,
I know that I am beautiful, and it's true,
And I hope that you can see it too.

PRIDE

Some people love girls, and some love boys,
Some love both, and that brings them joy,
Some don't feel like they fit in a box,
And that's okay, they don't have to stop.

It's important to remember, my dear,
That love is love, no matter who's near,
Whether it's a girl, boy, or non-binary friend,
Love knows no boundaries, it knows no end.

Some people may say that it's not right,
But it's important to stand up and fight,
For everyone deserves love and respect,
No matter who they love, or how they connect.

So let's embrace our differences, far and wide,
And let everyone love who they want to inside,
For the world is a better place, you'll see,
When we love each other, and live in harmony.

it's just a
BAD DAY
— not a —
BAD LIFE

Sometimes bad days come around,
And everything seems upside down,
The sun doesn't shine,
And things don't align,
And even your smile turns into a frown.

But remember that bad days won't stay,
They'll eventually go away,
And even though it seems tough,
And your road seems rough,
A better day will come, just you wait and see.

So if you're having a bad day,
Just keep on and don't lose your way,
You'll make it through, I know you will,
And tomorrow, you'll be smiling still.

The Disappointing Phone Call

There once was a telephone so fine,
It rang with a melodic chime,
But when it was answered,
It left one quite bothered,
As it was just a telemarketing line.

Unlikely Friends

An elephant and a monkey one day,
Met in the jungle, by the bay,
The monkey chattered and chattered away,
As the elephant listened, patiently, without sway.

The monkey was small, the elephant was grand,
But they got along, and walked hand in hand,
They laughed and played, until the day was done,
And they knew that their friendship had just begun.

So if a monkey and an elephant can be friends,
Then who's to say that friendship has any ends,
It's not about size, or color, or race,
It's about kindness and love, and a warm embrace.

The Dance of the Heart: A World Apart

With each step, she feels alive,
As her body begins to thrive,
In her heart, a rhythm beats,
And her soul begins to fleet.

With each turn, her worries fade,
As she glides, in a world self-made,
In her mind, a story unfolds,
And her spirit, it surely holds.

With each jump, she soars high,
As she dances, she reaches the sky,
In her body, a passion ignites,
And her senses come alive.

For the girl who loves to dance,
The world is but a stage to prance,
And with each move, she shares her heart,
As she dances, to a world apart.

...zzzz
BOO!
37

Monsters in my head, they growl and snarl,
Their voices taunting, making me feel small,
But I stand strong, I will not cower,
For I am the master of my own power.

With each breath, I chase them away,
I banish them to the light of day,
For they are just fears, and fears can't hurt,
I am in control, I won't be perturbed.

So if monsters in your head do lurk,
Remember, they're just shadows at work,
Stand tall, and let your light shine bright,
And chase those monsters out of sight.

Dance of Fireflies: A Magical Summer Evening

In the summer evening, just as the sun sets low
The dance of fireflies begins to glow.
A tiny flicker, a spark of light,
They rise and fall, taking flight.

A symphony of fireflies, dancing in the night,
With wings that shimmer, a magical sight.
A gentle breeze carries them on,
In the dark, they light up like a neon lawn.

The trees rustle with a quiet sound,
As the fireflies twirl round and round.
Their dance is graceful, their movement slow,
Their light like stars in the afterglow.

Children watch in wonder, their eyes bright,
As they see the fireflies' magical light.
They catch them in jars, watch them for a while,
Then release them back, with a gentle smile.

The dance of fireflies, a wondrous sight to see,
A moment of magic, for you and for me.
A reminder of nature's beauty and grace,
That we can find in the most unexpected place.

The Story Of
Bao & Pao

In a barnyard, not so far,
Lived a pig named Bao and a bird named Pao,
They may seem odd, an unlikely pair,
But their friendship was strong, beyond compare.

Bao was big, with a curly tail,
He loved to eat, and he loved to snort and wail,
Pao was small, with feathers so bright,
He loved to fly, soaring to new heights.

Bao would roll in the mud, all day long,
While Pao sang songs, with a melody so strong,
Bao would grunt, and Pao would chirp,
Together they made music, that could make the heart lurk.

One day, Bao was feeling blue,
He had lost his appetite, he didn't know what to do,
Pao saw his friend, in such distress,
He knew he had to act, to make things progress.

Pao gathered some worms, and flew to Bao's side,
He fed him the worms, with such pride,
Bao's eyes lit up, he was happy once more,
His friend Pao had lifted him up, off the floor.

From that day on, they were inseparable,
Their friendship grew stronger, it was undeniable,
Bao and Pao, an unlikely pair,
Their love and friendship, beyond compare.

In the barnyard, they roamed together,
Through thick and thin, through any weather,
Bao and Pao, an unlikely duo,
But their love and friendship, forever true.

Lynn Angela Rebello is a young author with a passion for creating stories that capture the hearts and imaginations of children. At just 17 years old, she has already shown a talent for weaving words together in a way that brings characters and worlds to life. Born and raised in a small town, Lynn's love of books and storytelling began at a young age. She has always been drawn to the magic and wonder of children's literature, and now she is excited to share her own stories with young readers around the world. In her spare time, Lynn enjoys exploring the outdoors, playing with her pets, and dreaming up new stories to tell. She hopes that her books will inspire children to embrace their creativity, follow their dreams, and always believe in themselves.

Welcome to a world of poetic wonder, where little ones can explore the beauty of gender equality, the importance of self-love, and the power of kindness. This collection of new age poetry is designed to spark the imagination of young minds while also introducing important values and life lessons. Through playful rhymes and colorful illustrations, children will discover the joy of embracing differences, treating others with respect, and loving themselves just as they are. With each poem, they will learn that they have the power to make a positive difference in the world around them, and that their voices matter. So come along on this magical journey, and let these poems inspire you to be the best version of yourself.

www.ingramcontent.com/pod-product-compliance
Lightning Source LLC
Chambersburg PA
CBHW050618160726
48003CB00003B/1239